AN I AM HEALING

WAVES of EMOTIONS

A Mindfulness Story

CHRISTY LYNN ANANA

Waves of Emotions
A Mindfulness Story
AN I AM HEALING SERIES BOOK
by Christy Lynn Anana

© 2023 Christy Lynn Anana

All rights reserved.

No part of this publication may be reproduced, stored in a retrieval system, or transmitted in any form or by any means, electronic, mechanical, photocopying, recording, or otherwise without the permission of the author.

Anana Press
ISBN: 978-1-957400-02-0
Illustrations by Shiraz Buhar, @sonabuhar, Fiverr.com
Cover and Interior design by Suzanne Fyhrie Parrott

ChristyLynnAnana.com

*Printed in the
United States of America*

Do you know that you have a

superhuman power?

You might not even realize

how powerful you are.

It's your awareness.

Aware of what?

Your feelings.

How do you know what you're feeling?

You are curious.

What do you notice?

Do you feel tightness in your throat? You might feel sad. Do you feel butterflies in your tummy? You might feel excitement or worry.

Do you feel relaxed or tense?

Do you hurt? Where?

Does your heart hurt?

What happened?

What can we do to help?

Need to talk?

Need a hug?

Want to go outside?

Or draw?

Need some time?

It's ok to not know what you need.

Feelings are like waves in the ocean.

They come and go.

You feel them and then they return to the sea.

Some are big and some are small.

The more you feel all the waves of the ocean, the better you'll get at handling anything that comes along.

Stay with the feeling

even when you want to

cry. Crying can help.

All your feelings are ok.

Read this book even when you feel good,

and then it will be natural to use your strategies.

Notice something you're feeling now.

Where does it live in your body?

Offer this practice for yourself so you feel better.

Take a deep breath and try to make

your exhalation very long.

Try it now.

Breathe in and bring your

shoulders up toward your ears.

Then, let your shoulders fall away

as you exhale deeply.

How does that feel?

Try it again.

If you feel comfortable,

let's go on a little relaxation

journey to help you feel better.

Imagine you are in a sturdy boat.

The waves gently rock you back and forth.

You feel safe in your boat as you steer your

way towards a little island.

You see birds flying above you.

You feel really cared for

and supported in your boat.

A little storm cloud floats by and rains

down on your head making your big

feelings move down your body.

Then, the sun replaces the cloud, and a

beautiful rainbow appears.

The rainbow points you to a place to dock.

You slip off your shoes and socks

and walk along the beach. You feel the wind in

your hair and the sun on your back.

You notice a beach house that

feels familiar and safe.

This place feels like home. One of your favorite

people is there, and they are so happy to see

you. You tell them about your adventures.

They laugh at the funny parts. They hug you

after you say something sad. You ask them for

words of advice that you need on your journey.

You listen to their good words.

Then you realize it is time to go.

You will have more adventures.

You tell your favorite person

that you will come back another time.

Maybe before you go to sleep tonight.

You say goodbye. You know you can come back to this place anytime you want. You walk along the beach. There is your boat waiting for you.

The rainbow appears again to show you the way back.

You hear the birds be happy to have you back on the journey.

You feel the waves move you up and down just like your breath.

Now, you know you're not alone.

You can connect with your people to help you.

It's going to get easier.

The more you feel all the waves of the ocean and breathe, the better you'll get at handling anything that comes along.

You get back on shore.

Feel your feet on the ground.

Breathe deeply.

Notice what you hear?

What do you see?

Any smells?

Tastes?

Touch your fingertips together.

I'm really proud of you. I hope you are proud of yourself. Thank you for going on this journey. Let's do it again.

Awareness of emotions is a skill and a practice. Even adults can get lost in a never-ending cycle of worries. By reading this book, Waves of Emotions, we build our emotional self-regulation. With mindfulness, we can connect, see things clearly, and get the help we need. When we do this work together, in partnership as a classroom or a family, we build onto our collective resiliency and social mindfulness.

ABOUT THIS STRATEGY

The breathing technique and guided visualization are resourcing techniques to bring about a sense of calm and safety.

Resourcing is a way to install coping skills so that you are able to deal with difficult emotions and feel better in the moment.

Check out more resources on YouTube @healingwithanana